SUFFOLK

A portrait in colour

MARK & ELIZABETH MITCHELS

COUNTRYSIDE BOOKS

Other counties in this series include:

BUCKINGHAMSHIRE
CHESHIRE
DERBYSHIRE
DEVON
DORSET
ESSEX
LANCASHIRE
LEICESTERSHIRE & RUTLAND
LINCOLNSHIRE
NORFOLK
NOTTINGHAMSHIRE
SHROPSHIRE
SURREY
SUSSEX
WARWICKSHIRE
WILTSHIRE

To our parents for their kindness and support
and to Barbara Hopkinson for making it all possible

First published 1993

This soft cover edition published 1999
Revised and updated 2004, 2007

COUNTRYSIDE BOOKS
3 CATHERINE ROAD
NEWBURY, BERKSHIRE

ISBN 1 85306 588 9

Produced through MRM Associates Ltd., Reading
Printed in Singapore

Contents

INTRODUCTION

Visitors come to Suffolk in search of the English dream of the countryside: fields ploughed by teams of strong but gentle Suffolk Punch, grasslands dotted with black-nosed Suffolk sheep and every river valley revealing pretty timber-framed cottages around a lofty flint built church. It may astonish them to discover how much of the idyll exists here in reality. It makes sense, then, to know that the term 'Silly Suffolk' was originally 'selig', meaning blessed or holy; and many will endorse the wisdom of past ages which bestowed such a name on this loveliest of counties.

Suffolk has over 500 medieval churches, more per square mile than any other county. In many villages these form the only point of contact with the past. When you sit in a church whose history stretches back over the centuries, you can begin to understand time. Look up to the roof and you will see exactly the same sight as a Victorian child, a Roundhead trooper or a medieval labourer. Time becomes manageable, and while the surroundings have perhaps changed out of all recognition, the people who have used the church have not. They laughed at the same things as we do, wept in the same way, loved and hated with the same intensity and believed they were unique. Churches have survived so far because they have been wanted. Dwindling congregations may mean that eventually churches are abandoned, left to crumble and become overgrown.

In this they will join the other ways of life which are no more: the weavers and clothiers who traded their skills and wares throughout Europe and built up enormous fortunes, some of which they gave back to the church to save their eternal souls; the great fishing fleets which gathered in the harvest of the North Sea until with biblical enormity they found they had landed all there was to catch; the hundreds of thousands of unknown farm labourers who toiled from dawn to dusk in all weathers, trudging home in time only to eat and sleep before the next day's progress towards a pauper's grave. Perhaps the village as a unit itself will die, rendered unnecessary by the dual carriageway and computer work stations!

This may sound unlikely, but then so did the demise of the wool trade. Wool was for many centuries the source of the nation's wealth, and Suffolk had an importance out of all proportion to its size. It produced more cloth than any other part of Britain, and ensured that a few of its citizens were among the richest. These men employed whole communities to produce high quality broadcloth which sold throughout Europe. They were all-powerful in their towns and villages, and their houses and guildhalls were deliberately intended to be statements of their wealth and importance. In the 1550s the wool trade suffered an enormous blow: fashion moved on, and the demand for Suffolk's cloth fell. The influx of highly skilled weavers from the Netherlands gave the industry a new lease of life, but they settled in the larger towns, leaving the older centres to specialize in silk weaving (at Hadleigh, Glemsford and Boxford, for instance) while others turned their energies towards less glamorous textiles made from horse-hair and coconut fibres. The 19th century improvements and inventions required fast-flowing water or steam power; the great manufacturing towns of the north were born, and, bereft of work and money, the old wool towns returned slowly to the occupations of the land. The old buildings aged gracefully and found new roles, seemingly content to await their rediscovery in our own time; but their preservation is perhaps at the expense of 21st century vitality, for unemployment and high house prices have conspired to drive out the next generation of truly local people. Holiday and weekend cottages continue to attract city dwellers, who take advantage of the ever-improving road system into the county. Chief among these must be the A14 which exists to connect the container port of Felixstowe with the Midlands.

There are 50 miles of coastline in Suffolk, and it lacks so many things we regard as essential, such as easy communications and non-stop entertainment, that by rights it should have few friends. In fact it is a popular Heritage coast, with bird reserves at Minsmere and Havergate Island, coastal walks from Bawdsey up to Covehithe and rivers which are amongst the most unspoilt n the land. At either end of the county the resort ports of Felixstowe and Lowestoft are sure proof that Suffolk can adapt when it needs to.

Ipswich was one of the earliest Anglo-Saxon settlements, and from the first was a port which traded with European centres, as it still does today. Recent excavations have revealed that the old street plan has been adhered to, and the street names themselves remind us of their distinguished past. The medieval town was rich in churches and merchants, some evidence of which has survived the improvements and mistakes of later centuries. This was the birthplace of Cardinal Wolsey, chief minister to the young Henry VIII, and he hoped to transform Ipswich into a university city to stand beside Oxford and Cambridge. His greed exceeded his grasp of reality, for he crossed his king and lost, dying en route to London and a trial for treason. Only the sad gateway to St Peter's Church beside the harbour marks the building plans he had in mind.

Artists, musicians, writers and all seekers for that personal something, have found in Suffolk the calm and breadth of perspective that is essential in these hectic times. It is a debt readily acknowledged by the most sensitive of creative talents: Gainsborough confessed, 'Suffolk made me a painter', while Constable, echoing his compatriot, wrote of his inspiration to a friend: 'I associate my careless boyhood with all that lies on the banks of the Stour. They made me a painter, and I am grateful . . . I love every stile and stump, and every lane in the village, so deep rooted are early impressions.' In 1951 Britten told an audience: 'I am firmly rooted in this glorious county. And I proved this to myself when I once tried to live somewhere else.' For many people in Suffolk these words express their own feelings towards this beautiful county.

Woodbridge

Although the town of Woodbridge can trace its existence back to Saxon times, its growth and importance date from the late medieval period. As the skills of the shipwrights were developed, the need for proper ports and quaysides became unavoidable, and towns like Woodbridge were quick to respond. The harbour made some men rich, and they chose to show their gratitude and faith by endowing the church. The superb tower of St Mary's Church dominates the river approach as it has done since 1450.

Once there had been an abbey in Woodbridge. When Thomas Seckford, Master of the Court of Requests to Elizabeth I, became the owner of the abbey ruins, he ushered in a time of change and improvement, the evidence of which still surrounds and benefits the townspeople. He built a grand brick town house, and in 1575 he established the Shire Hall, which stands on Market Hill, complete with his crest over the stairways, and two tiny lock-up cells beneath them. Not content with this generosity, he established at his death in 1587 almshouses for the deserving poor which survive to this day. In the 19th century the income from his charity was sufficient to rebuild them on a grander scale, and the old grammar school was allowed to benefit from the income as well. The name of Seckford continues to play a large part in the town's life.

The Tide Mill is the most famous building in the town, and offers an insight into the past, which our present energy-conscious time might reconsider. It uses the natural action of the tide to fill a pond which drives a mill wheel – twice a day, every day. The present mill building dates from 1793, and was working until 1957 when the main shaft broke. Today it has been restored and is working once again, although the original mill pond is now a marina. It is a popular tourist attraction, and artists cannot resist its appeal.

Traffic has taken its toll on the narrow streets, but many interesting buildings have survived. The Bell and Steelyard Inn in New Street dates from the 17th century and includes a curious weighing machine which could cope with farm carts in their entirety! The fact that New Street is 450 years old says a lot for this town, which has retained a pleasing sense of proportion, and a stubborn resilience in the face of unnecessary modernism.

tom

Kersey

One of the most remarkable aspects of a visit to this prettiest of Suffolk villages, is that somehow it manages to look as though it has yet to be discovered. However often it appears in tourist brochures, television documentaries or – dare I say – in books like this, it nevertheless contrives to exclude everything which is modern or offensive. Countless thousands of visitors have walked an identical route from the church down to the Splash, and from there on up the other side, and once again turned to marvel at the unspoilt perfection of a true rural idyll – but of their passing there is nothing. Like sand, the village covers everything it does not wish to see, and it is our very anonymity which ensures its survival. Some countries would have declared such a place a national museum, moved out the real residents, and bussed in theme-park actors to perform upon a rustic stage, but not so in Kersey. The village lives, and as the last of the day's tourists pack away the cameras and guide books before driving back to depressing reality, the heart resumes its beat behind the attractive façades, and life flows on as it has done for centuries. Perhaps that is really the saddest truth: a hundred years ago Kersey was pretty, but not unique, and now it is both. In fairness to history, the comforts of the modern day would have eased the plight of those poor folk who slaved for a pittance on the heavy soils which surround this settlement, and who are now sleeping in the churchyard.

It was wool which brought wealth to Kersey, and the village gave its name to a tough, workmanlike cloth. It is both foolish and pointless to attempt to explain why Kersey is so pretty: if you need proof, stay away! However, we all have an image in our mind of English village life, and Kersey does match most of the ingredients. The church of St Mary stands on a hill overlooking the houses, like a shepherd above his flock. A flight of stone steps leads down to the first cottages, and one after another the houses seem to vie with each other for perfection. Tiny cottages, pretty shops and impressive farm houses, they all rub shoulders and combine their charms into one glorious experience. The Splash with its friendly families of wildfowl is the focal point, and artists cannot resist the challenge of its views. The nearby former Priory, with its elaborate red brick chimneys, seems almost impertinent, so great is the fund of timber treasures available. The Bell Inn, conscious of its need to please and welcome, is bedecked with flowers and offers an excuse to stay a little longer away from the present, bustling age! Sadly the last shop in the village has recently closed its doors for good, bringing to an end years of sturdy independence. The final view must be of the village nestling in the High Suffolk valley, its weathered roofs and chimneys utterly unchanged, and the church on guard at the entrance. If there is a village time forgot, then Kersey is a vivid reminder of it.

Newmarket

In 1605 King James I came to Newmarket to enjoy some hawking and hare coursing, but ended up racing horses. Over the years his heirs continued to visit this Suffolk town, and established it as the headquarters of British horse racing – the sport of kings.

It is estimated that every year about 110,000 thoroughbred foals are born throughout the world: all of them could be traced back to just three progenitors – Byerley Turk, Darley and Godolphin Arab. In the 17th and 18th centuries breeding produced magnificent racing horses, and the stock has never been permitted to suffer. At Newmarket is the National Stud which maintains records of all the thoroughbreds and their histories. Some of the finest horses in the world enjoy its 500 acres of pasture.

Racing soon acquired many rules which in time came to be defined and upheld by the Jockey Club. In 1772 a grand residence was built in the High Street, still easily distinguished by its stately lantern. Everything except gambling debts was within their remit; this not unimportant aspect of racing was left to Tattersalls, who built the New Subscription Rooms next door in 1844, enabling them to combine horse auctions with the settlements of wagers. This building is now the National Horseracing Museum. Here the visitor is taken on a tour which includes the stories of the sport's legendary horses, famous riders, trainers and owners and a display of the skeleton of *Eclipse,* foaled in 1764, who after a spectacular career on the turf went on to sire the winners of 862 races!

Almost any morning it is possible to walk out to the Moulton Road Heath and see hundreds of horses exercising, as they have done for centuries. Long lines of mounts walk to and from the town, their riders occasionally smarting from the harsh words snapped out by trainers and head lads. Then without warning a group will break into a gallop and the thunder of hooves on the heath provides the authentic sound of Newmarket. It is said that there are over 20 miles of white fencing surrounding the town. The stables nestle within, and pretty suburban streets can reveal behind a brick arch the courtyard and stalls of another famous name. The Earl of Bath in 1753 acknowledged the importance of trainers and jockeys, noting 'it is sometimes observed that the race is won as much by the dexterity of the rider, as by the vigour and fleetness of the animal.' At either end of the wide High Street there are monuments incorporating equine imagery. Everything gives way to horses, including the internal combustion engine, which always comes a poor second. Until 1967, even the railway station employed a horse to shunt wagons!

The odd thing about Newmarket is that the county boundary encircles the town, cutting off the race course – which actually lies in Cambridgeshire . . .

Flatford Mill & Willy Lott's Cottage

Suffolk can lay claim to two of Britain's most brilliant artists: Thomas Gainsborough, a native of Sudbury, one of our greatest portraitists; and John Constable, who was born in 1776 in the village of East Bergholt, on the Suffolk-Essex border. Constable's landscapes are widely regarded as representing the perfect English countryside: rich, rolling farmland, valleys shaded by aged trees, with agricultural workers quietly pursuing their tasks. But this was no idyllic dream stemming from a fertile imagination: the scenes Constable depicted were firmly rooted in the reality of the Stour valley near his home.

John's father, Golding, was a wealthy corn merchant, running watermills at Flatford and Dedham, and farming 93 acres. John showed early artistic talent, taking his inspiration from the countryside, and wanting to make 'a pure and unaffected representation of the scenes'. Even when he had moved to London to pursue his studies in art, he returned in spring and summer to his native village, spending his time wandering through the valley making tiny pencil studies or oil sketches which he would then work up into larger paintings in his studio in London. On one of these return visits to Suffolk he met the granddaughter of the local Rector, Maria Bicknell; their engagement met with family disapproval and, although they were finally married in 1816, they enjoyed only twelve happy years together before, weakened by tuberculosis and the birth of their seventh child, Maria died. Ironically, within months her husband attained the elusive professional success which her family had sought – he was elected to the Royal Academy.

Constable's *The Hay Wain* is the most frequently reproduced of all British paintings. It shows Gibeon's Farm, the home of Willy Lott, which stands close to Flatford Mill on the Stour. Willy Lott was an eccentric who claimed delicate health prevented him from leaving the farm; but he lived well into his eighties! Constable's painting, about 4' by 6', took five months to complete and was shown in 1821 at the Royal Academy. It was one of a series of paintings of the Stour valley which Constable undertook; these include several of the Mill itself, the lock and the surrounding Dedham Vale. In 1832, while travelling through the area, he remarked on the beauty of the scene and was told, 'Yes, sir; this is Constable's country' – a fitting tribute to perhaps our greatest landscape painter.

Orford Castle

In the world of make-believe, we always imagine that if we could live in another age, we would be one of the great and the good, comfortably surrounded by servants and gracious living. Well, any hopes that life in a medieval castle would meet these requirements are cruelly shattered by a tour of Orford Castle. Life in its stone keep must have been awful, and only the direct threats to safety must have enforced residence! From the moment of passing through the main doorway there is a sharp drop in temperature, and the eyes have to adjust to the gloom. Leading off from the central hall are various chambers, serving as kitchen and chaplain's room, which are hollowed out of the actual walls. The chapel is a bit better, having a couple of reasonable windows, but even here the warlike purpose of the place is paramount, for the portcullis rose up the wall through a hole in the floor when not in use. The upper hall follows a similar design, except that the wall cavities are now apartments for the Constable and other officers. Add to the gloom and cold the smell from the wall-discharging latrines, and the attractions of castle life pale. And this is without the possibility of death or injury – for above all Orford Castle was a building for war.

King Henry II had good reason to distrust the mighty Bigod family, who controlled this part of Suffolk out of Framlingham Castle. He chose to check-mate them by building a castle on the coast at Orford which would defy any local threats, and prevent reinforcements arriving by sea. The keep has 18 sides, and stands 30 metres high, giving an unrivalled view over the countryside, and a commanding position of the port and all seaborne vessels. A curtain wall completed the castle, which cost the King £1,413 9 shillings and 2 pence. Within a year a rebellion in East Anglia obliged it to uphold the Crown's cause.

The town grew and thrived in the shelter of the castle, but the coastline was constantly shifting, and by Tudor times the port was suffering as a great shingle spit advanced south, forming a navigation hazard which curtailed the town's prosperity. Today the spit (called Orford Ness and now in the custody of the National Trust) continues for miles down the coast, resulting in the creation of the river Ore. The quayside now provides a mooring for pleasure craft, and the main street has rather too quaint cottages which once were the only home of hard-working fishermen. Oysters are still famous local fare here, along with smoked herring, and many visitors sample both in an excellent restaurant off the market place.

In 1165, as the castle was being built, a strange creature was hauled from the sea, and taken under guard to the King's officer. It was neither man nor fish, and did not respond to torture! Eventually it was able to escape, and has never been seen again. The legend of the Merman is still strong in these parts, and if it ever does emerge again from the cold waters of the North Sea, it is unlikely it will feel itself drawn to the gaunt, cold tower which has surveyed the coast since its last appearance.

Beccles

'A well built and improving market town'. So Beccles was described 150 years ago, and the verdict of today's visitor would no doubt be much the same, for although much has happened in its long history, the town has adapted to contemporary life with common sense and enthusiasm.

Beccles owes much to its situation, 25 miles from the sea on the navigable river Waveney, and set on rising ground commanding the marshy plain which stretches into Norfolk. Once wherries could sail as far as Bungay, and Beccles Quay was busy with their cargoes. It was an important herring port, and The Score, a narrow lane opposite the old market, was used to bring the fish up from the riverside. Despite the townspeople's schemes, the river silted up and the focus of commerce shifted. Now the river traffic is of Broadland cruisers, thousands of which moor every year at the Staithe; for Beccles is linked not only to Oulton Broad, Lowestoft and the sea, but also to the greater Broads system in Norfolk. The waterfront is attractive, with parks and open spaces. To the eastern side of the new bridge which takes much of the heavy traffic away from Beccles town centre, the river is bordered by the town Common or Fen – reclaimed marshes, once amounting to 1,400 acres, and given by a charter of Elizabeth I to the townspeople who used its reeds for thatching, turf for fuel and the land for grazing. A two day race meeting used to be held here; later the 'Frolic' enlivened the Quay with its swimming and sailing races. Nowadays the Carnival and Regatta in August attract visitors, and the Quay is being developed as a focal point, with sporting and leisure facilities.

Market days in Beccles see an influx of shoppers from the surrounding district. New Market, at the top of the hill, was established in medieval times, replacing the old Saxon market place which now acts as the bus station. Modern shops and supermarkets abound, but the street plan is very old, and the names are resonant of those times: Blyburgate, Puddingmoor, Sheepgate. Dominating New Market is the tower of the church of St Michael, 97 feet high and containing a peal of ten bells. It is, unusually, separate from its church. St Michael's has a beautifully decorated south porch; not only that, but its position overlooking the flat land of south Norfolk, crisscrossed with drainage ditches and grazed by cattle, together with the colour and activity of the cruisers, make this a spectacular panorama.

Beccles has suffered catastrophic fires, and most of the finer buildings are Georgian. In Northgate, 17th century red brick Dutch gabled houses with splendid gardens overlook the river. The King's Head Inn is an old coaching inn, overlooking the market place, and the old Free School, founded by Sir John Leman in the 17th century, still stands in Puddingmoor. But Beccles is by no means a museum piece; its industry is inconspicuous and the town itself has over 100 clubs and societies of all kinds, and remains a lively centre for this part of Suffolk.

PATTON
F889

The Harvest of the Sea

Fishing has been more than a source of income to the people who live beside the temperamental North Sea: it has been a way of life. In the boom years before the First World War 1,600 steam drifters operated out of the East Coast ports and on any single night the sea would reflect the myriad coloured lights of 300 fishing boats, moving in silent procession through the night, harvesting the seemingly inexhaustible shoals of herring.

At the end of the exceptional autumn of 1913, Lowestoft had landed an incredible quantity of herring. Forty railway wagons of fish departed for London every hour. Europe, and in particular Germany, was the main market. Of course, today we know these great fleets fished the herring to the point of extinction. As a sort of atonement the Government has for a long time had the laboratories of the Department of Environment, Food and Rural Affairs (DEFRA) at Lowestoft, working to prevent such catastrophic over-fishing recurring.

Now that the modern fishing boat can cost as much as a quarter of a million pounds, perhaps it is not surprising that there are far fewer of them. A sign of the changing times in indicated by the number of orange-painted boats which support the North Sea gas and oil platforms.

There are still smaller, inshore fishing boats at work along the Suffolk coast like this one pictured at Walberswick, and places like Bawdsey, Aldeburgh and Dunwich sell the freshest fish possible – indeed, you can literally buy it from the still dripping boat. At Lowestoft these boats use squid for their bait, and there is no better example of the changes which have transformed the industry that the fact that it comes all the way from the Falkland Islands!

Helmingham Hall

Every evening since the year 1510 both of the drawbridges at Helmingham Hall have been raised, leaving the wide, deep moat to ensure the privacy and security of the Tollemache family for another night! It was in 1487 that the family came to this part of Suffolk, a few miles north of Ipswich, and soon afterwards they pulled down the first house to make way for an altogether grander statement. Originally the Hall was built in the half-timbered style, but subsequent building improvements have altered the exterior appearance to the one seen today. At first glance it may seem that the Hall is wholly of brick construction, but in reality the upper half of the wall comprises thin tiles, hung from the original timber framework. It is the combination of warm brickwork, elegant white windows and delightfully varied chimney pieces which make the Hall so pleasing to the eye. The moat, with its two iron bridges, is well stocked with fish, and in former days was even the source of the water supply!

The gardens of the Hall are open to the public. These include a kitchen garden which provides all the traditional fruits, vegetables and herbs, and a parterre garden. The main garden is divided into four large beds, after the Elizabethan style, and each has a surrounding herbaceous border. At the entrance to the beautiful formal garden is a wrought iron gate, its piers surmounted by the Tollemache crest. A moat encircles this area and it is believed to be all that remains of the original Saxon hall. Wherever the visitor wishes to walk there are flowers, shrubs and bushes, complemented by graceful statuary and the backdrop of the Hall itself.

In the 400 acres of parkland, large herds of red and fallow deer graze freely, as they have done for centuries, and also herds of Highland cattle and wild sheep. Today there are safari rides available around the estate to see the animals. The woodlands of Helmingham were famous for supplying the shipyards of Woodbridge, and the artist John Constable painted a scene in the park showing one such tree, twisting away from the river's edge. The tree can still be seen today. An impressive avenue of oak trees, some of them over 300 years old, lines the main approach to the house.

Within the park is the church of St Mary which was begun in 1488, and contains the Tollemache memorials. The lakes, or Leys, are crossed by a pretty bridge, and like so many places, provide a home for wildlife. But, as Tollemache intended, it is the Hall itself which is the focal point of the park. Although its appearance has changed considerably, the essential impact of a moated country house remains impressive. Queen Elizabeth I stayed here twice, and the present Queen has also been a visitor – a sure sign that this wonderful property is truly in a class of its own.

Saxtead Green Windmill

A windmill is one of those indisputably traditional buildings. It appears to complete an English landscape, in the same way as a church steeple - and for the same reason. It harks back to an age of simplicity, innocence and perfection. Today we cannot hope to understand much of the sophisticated technology which surrounds us, but there was a time when the windmill marked the limits of man's achievement.

The first reference to a windmill at Saxtead is in 1287, and the accounts which have survived show that the carpenters were paid 73 shillings, and the mill stones increased the cost by 33 shillings. These were considerable amounts of money and emphasize just how important a venture the construction would have been. Bread was the basic foodstuff, and the deplorable state of the roads meant that every village would need to be able to mill its own grain. Sometimes a community would have several mills, and then the competition would be very fierce, and perhaps even a bit unpleasant. The miller was clearly an important person in any village, but the popular perception of him was that he cheated his customers at every opportunity. Chaucer's *Canterbury Tales* has a famous portrait of a miller, and the tricks of the trade may amuse us, but to the starving peasants his theft of their food source must have been galling, to say the least. Perhaps the Saxtead miller was different, and went out of his way to ensure he accounted for all the grain he milled!

The present mill dates from 1796 and worked until 1947. It represents the very peak of the art of mill construction, and it is extraordinary that a building which is functional in every respect, should at the same time be so aesthetically satisfying. Conditions inside must have been uncomfortable, even dangerous. The great central post and the machinery it drives have priority, so the miller had to squeeze himself around it. The grain was stored in bins in the roof, and gravity sent it through the machinery. This was an extremely dusty business, and today's visitor can enjoy the climb and the views, while the miller probably just longed for a thirst quencher!

It is a post mill, which means it can be turned to keep the sails square to the wind. In this case it sits on a brick round house, which served as a store. The white boarded upper section is approached by alarmingly steep stairs, which have to travel round as well. The sophistication of the present design is that the wind would not only work the millstones inside, but also power the sack hoist. Inside there are two pairs of stones, driven by the enormous sails, which have a total span of 55 feet. The great fan tail which rises from the stairway keeps the mill into the wind at all times.

Today Saxtead Green Mill is in the care of English Heritage and the visitor can enjoy a full tour of the building, and appreciate its workings with the help of the excellent information boards which are on display everywhere.

Minsmere Nature Reserve

This award-winning reserve is one of the great success stories of the Suffolk coast. Once poor farming land reclaimed from marsh, it was flooded as a defence measure during the last war, and shortly afterwards a pair of nesting avocets were spotted here – returning to this country after an absence of 100 years. The RSPB first leased, then bought the land. Now, together with its sister reserve Havergate Island just to the south, it has established a record for the successful breeding of avocets, and careful management has encouraged the return of other rare species. The reserve covers 2,000 acres of a prime site, on the migratory routes of many birds; but its chief attraction is the variety of habitats it affords. There are areas of woodland with deciduous trees such as oak and birch: woodpecker, nuthatch, redstart and sparrowhawk nest here, and up to 60 pairs of nightingales. The open scrubland known as the Suffolk Sandlings was grazed by sheep and then by rabbits until the 1950s; ground cover is provided by bracken, heather and gorse, and scattered trees encourage nightjars. The marshland is a mass of whispering reeds which hide the nests of endangered species like marsh harriers and bitterns. On the coastal side of the reserve, the shallow lagoons known as The Scrape are rich in shrimps and larvae which feed waders such as sandpipers and ruff, and during the nesting season areas of pebbly beach have to be cordoned off to allow little tern to breed in peace.

For the human visitor, access is along narrow, winding roads through the estate and, once at the heart of the reserve, the wildlife takes first priority. Walkers must keep to the signposted trails. These take varied routes, each covering about two miles; the focal point is the hides. There are eight of these, some in the woods, but most centred upon The Scrape. These 55 acres – artificially created some 30 years ago by bulldozers – are a haven for wildfowl and waders. Here you may well observe the famous avocets, or as many as 30 other species.

And there is more than just birds; moths and butterflies, bats and dragonflies, squirrels, otter and adders may be found here. Plants include orchids and fungi, some of them poisonous. But do not think of the reserve as a place where nature goes unchecked; there are predators, such as deer, foxes and gulls, which have to be discouraged, and the management works throughout the year to create and maintain the most attractive conditions for important species: bracken and gorse are cleared, and the balance of fresh and salt water maintained by a series of sluices. The reserve attracts some 70,000 visitors a year. Some are mere amateurs, desirous of a quiet day in this restful place. Others are true 'twitchers' who come in search of a glossy ibis or a bee-eater blown off course by freak winds, or trying to beat the record of 109 different species spotted in a single day.

Lowestoft

Within living memory the port of Lowestoft was thronged; every autumn, thousands of sail or steam drifters arrived in Lowestoft, having sailed down the East Coast from the Shetlands, following the shoals of migrating herring. On the shore, a vast army of Scottish girls followed the boats, gutting, curing and packing the fish for the markets, and a whole host of dependent trades thrived – chandlers, rope-makers, coopers. Now only a few dozen trawlers fish from Lowestoft, and their catches are of plaice and cod. In the heady days of prosperity just before the First World War, it was impossible to imagine the perils of overfishing, but the herring shoals have been ruined, and modern bureaucracy means that the trawlers' catches are limited by Common Market quotas. A whole way of life has disappeared. To remind us of how wealthy the fishing industry once was, we have the *Lydia Eva*.

This little boat, the last steam drifter in the world, was built in 1930 and fished from Great Yarmouth. She was launched by the lady shown in the picture below – Lydia Eva. During the Second World War she was taken over by the RAF, and she was eventually rescued in the 1980s and restored to working condition, becoming at the same time a museum and a memorial to the men of the East Coast herring fisheries.

Nowadays many of the sailing craft in Lowestoft are supply ships for the offshore oil and gas fields, so the port area is still busy. Fresh fish is landed daily and sold locally or dispatched to London, and it is interesting to join a tour of the Fish Market. The Maritime Museum in Sparrow's Nest Park tells the history of the town's principal industry with evocative displays and mementos. Lowestoft is also the headquarters for the Directorate of Fisheries Research, which seeks ways of preserving fish stocks and improving the marine environment.

On nearby Oulton Broad, sailing of a different kind is to be seen, when the national powerboat championships take place. The town is divided by the river Waveney, which flows from Oulton Broad through Lake Lothing and under the renowned swing bridge. To the north lie the port and most of the larger shops. To the south are the beach and the seafront gardens, with many opportunities for leisure and recreation. South Beach, with its fine, white sand, has won awards for its cleanliness and safety.

LT63
LT 63
ST NICOLA

Hadleigh

The main roads hereabouts indicate 'Hadleigh – an historic town' – and so indeed it is. Hadleigh has a long and distinguished past, all the more interesting because so much of it remains for the modern visitor to enjoy. Certainly there are few surviving monuments from those ancient days when Hadleigh was a Viking royal town, the seat of King Guthrum in the 9th century – the tomb in the church purporting to be his proves to be no older than medieval; but the prosperity of Hadleigh as a wool town in the Middle Ages is there for all to see, in the well preserved buildings all around. In the High Street, for instance, about a third of the houses and shops are clearly ancient, dating from the years of prosperity before the 1600s; but many more have had merely the façade brought up to date, and medieval, Georgian and Victorian stand next to each other with their diverse building styles and materials. Many are colourwashed in yellow, white or Suffolk pink, and have outstanding examples of pargetting – raised designs in plasterwork. Sometimes these show fairly simple patterns, but in Hadleigh you will find more freely drawn decorations, including flowers and family crests. The best examples are in the High Street, which runs almost parallel to the river Brett for about three quarters of a mile. The river is the key to Hadleigh's wealth, since it provided power, water to wash the wool and full the cloth, and access to the ports. In its heyday as many as 1,500 townspeople were involved in the wool trade (their speciality was in making crêpe) and they had sufficient funds to build splendid houses for themselves, as well as to embellish and enlarge the splendid church of St Mary. This stands just off the High Street in a tranquil setting – an interesting contrast with its erstwhile importance as the hub of commercial activity, because opposite is the beautiful Guildhall, whose central section was the old market hall. This unusual three storeyed building was provided for the town by the wealthy clothier William de Clopton in 1438 and rented to them at a cost of one red rose per annum; the custom of placing a red rose on de Clopton's tomb in Long Melford church has recently been revived. De Clopton lived in the nearby Toppesfield Hall, which is now the headquarters of the East Anglia Tourist Board. The Deanery Tower next to the churchyard is a Tudor gatehouse (1495), part of a larger building project which was never completed, but notable nonetheless as the place where the Oxford Movement started in 1833. A pleasant walk along the river Brett shows other examples of Hadleigh's industry: the old silk mill, where children as young as eight years old were once employed, and to the north the old maltings, which have been beautifully converted into the offices of Babergh District Council. Hadleigh is an important administrative centre, with a busy commercial life – the market is held on Tuesdays and Fridays – and it is justifiably proud of its heritage.

1618
99

Dunwich

'The sea then overtook a third part of the town, and so enfeebled the haven by storm and tempest that it closes up once or twice a year.' Those words, written in 1300, pin-point the moment when a great port and town realised it was doomed to disappear beneath the sea. Today, the remains of Dunwich are only revealed to intrepid divers as they pick their way over the sea bed. It is a sobering tale of pride coming before a mighty fall, and has a clear message for our own ecologically sensitive times.

There was a town at Dunwich in Roman times, and during the Anglo-Saxon period it rose to become an important trading port and ecclesiastical centre. By the time of the Norman Conquest and the Domesday Book it was the largest of the six Suffolk boroughs, and Ipswich was an inferior second. To an extent its prosperity was based not just on its endeavours as a port, but on its fortunate geographical location: it commanded a river mouth, which gave the smaller ports of Blythburgh, Walberswick and Southwold access to the sea. They had to pay their dues at Dunwich Haven, and received no favours; indeed the animosity arising from their sense of injustice was to prove a key factor when Dunwich found itself in difficulty.

Even kings were grateful for its favours – Dunwich supplied many of the ships which conveyed medieval armies to wars in France. But the business of Dunwich was business. Shipbuilding and other associated trades ensured that the merchants and mariners of the town could embark on their dangerous, uncertain but profitable voyages. From Iceland came fish, furs and timber, while the Low Countries exported cloth and France shipped wine. Historians cannot agree as to the size of Dunwich at its peak, but all agree there were many parishes within the great town wall.

The harbour was formed behind a long shingle spit which was known as Kingsholme, and which was inexorably extending southwards. The harbour mouth was vulnerable to storm damage from the time of the 13th century. In 1220 the harbour was almost closed, and by 1286 the records show that a severe storm overwhelmed the coastal defences and destroyed two of the coastal parishes. Worse followed, for in 1328 the court was informed: 'On January 14th in the first year of the present King (Edward III) there was a certain port, by the force of the sea, it was completely blocked.' If this was indeed Dunwich it proved to be the final blow, for it was impossible to reopen the harbour to ships, and the population moved out, leaving the streets, churches and houses to the wrath of the North Sea. Gradually the coastline assumed the form it has today, and the once proud borough slipped beneath the waves. Today a few pieces of wall and a couple of sad flint arches remain. They say the bells of long lost churches can be heard beneath the waves on a stormy night. Stand on the cliffs and look out to sea, and you want that story to be true, for this is a unique place that deserves a chilling legend.

River Orwell

There are few places along the length of this beautiful river which do not have at least a passing association with smuggling, which in the 18th and early 19th centuries would seem to have reached epidemic proportions. The most famous smuggler of them all was Margaret Catchpole, who seems to have enjoyed her work, and passed from history into legend, by way of a famous novel. She is supposed to have involved her sweetheart William Laud in the business when they met in The Ship Inn at Levington. Overlooking Woolverstone marina is Cat House, named after Margaret's clever signal, whereby a stuffed cat in the window indicated that the preventive men were about. She must have worked hard, for her name occurs in many village stories, but at length she was caught; while Laud was shot, she died in 1819 having served her sentence in Australia.

In 1553 the landlord of the Butt and Oyster at Pin Mill obtained a licence to run his pub, and was among the very first to do so for that was the year licensing began. Since that time, this spot on the river has been a favourite with every generation. It is famous for the old working barges which used to tie up here, but now they are remembered at the annual Barge Match when enthusiasts bring their lovingly restored craft to Pin Mill to show them off, and enjoy the company. This is the only Suffolk pub to have been featured regularly in the *Good Beer Guide*. At any time of the year it is a lovely spot, and feels gloriously remote. Arthur Ransome had a cottage here, and when he moved down from the Lake District, the carrier protested he could not delay his return, as he must get back to England!

Higher up the river old and new come together as the modern achievement of the Orwell Road Bridge sweeps past lonely Freston Tower. Dating from the 16th century, this six storey brick tower is said to have been built to serve the educational needs of the owner's daughter Ellen: on Mondays she studied good works on the ground floor, and daily ascended the floors accompanied by weaving, music, classics, literature and painting, until she appropriately embraced astronomy on the roof every Sunday.

The river Orwell may have thriving marinas at Shotley, Levington, Woolverstone and Ipswich, but it is still an important commercial route, as Ipswich continues to trade with Europe via the sea, and vessels of up to 9,000 tons can make their way up the river at high tide.

Lavenham

The march of progress has left us with very few complete towns which offer a glimpse of a bygone age, and there are none to rival Lavenham, for it is a perfectly preserved medieval wool centre of the sort which once abounded in East Anglia. Here are no isolated timber houses, jostled by modern concrete and glass, but whole streets and courtyards formed by English oak and Suffolk craftsmanship. There are over 300 listed buildings. To stand anywhere in this town is to marvel at the sheer number of surviving bits of English history – for this is merry England as it should be. Overlooking Lavenham is the magnificent church of St Peter and St Paul.

How did it survive? Lavenham's prosperity was founded on wool, and in the Middle Ages that meant skilled craftsmen working on looms in their own houses. There were no factories, and no powered machines. On the edge of the town were the fields teeming with sheep and in the

houses were the people who transformed the wool into bales of high quality cloth. For centuries the conditions were ideal. But the inventions of the 18th century improved cloth manufacture at Lavenham's expense: machines were driven by steam, and that meant coal. Within a few generations the wool trade had collapsed. The old industrial centre gently adjusted its pace, and soon became a market town, with agriculture as its chief employer. Times were hard, and buildings were expensive to alter, so the old wool workshops remained essentially unchanged. Now the business of the town is inseparable from tourism, and preservation makes sound economic sense.

The Guildhall has dominated Market Place, as it was meant to do, since it was built in 1529. Here the town's wool magnificoes would have consolidated their wealth, power and importance. From their windows they would have seen the trading and dealing in full progress around the simple Market Cross, confident that nothing could displace Lavenham's status.

Small streets emanate from the centre, and each has more than its fair share of pretty timber buildings. Perhaps one reason why we like the houses is that we can appreciate their construction at a glance, and perhaps imagine we could knock one up – given the wood and a good saw! De Vere House, the Priory, the Swan Inn – seemingly countless gems await the pedestrian's gaze, and they are all unique.

The Crooked House

Bungay & The River Waveney

The quiet river Waveney rises near Diss, in a patch of boggy ground called Redgrave Fen, home of the Great Raft Spider and a Site of Special Scientific Interest. The river flows almost due east, and for most of its length it forms the border between Norfolk and Suffolk. It is a slow, meandering river which has a tendency in winter to flood the level plain, so the main road keeps to the higher ground on the Norfolk side. The first town of any size on the Waveney is Bungay, with a population of about 5,000. This is an ancient town built where the river loops northwards, forming a horse-shoe shape occupied by Outney Common, with Bungay in the defensible position where the tongue of land narrows. The town was on the old Roman Stone Street, and had Saxon earthbank fortifications. In the 12th century Roger Bigod, a supporter of William the Conqueror and one of the greatest landowners of East Anglia, built a castle here, and the remains of fortifications can still be seen. Eventually the castle had to be surrendered to the king and destroyed, but part of the walls – once 18 feet thick – and the enormous towers remain. From the Castle Meadows there are lovely views over the water meadows, and from here starts the Bigod Way, a network of walks in and around Bungay, with such picturesque names as Constitution Stroll, Rabbitskin Run and Bath Hills Walk, which takes you to where there was indeed once a cold water bath in the days when this was a spa town. Bungay has few really ancient buildings, apart from the churches: Holy Trinity with its round flint knapped tower dates from about 1000 AD; and the church of St Mary, alas, now redundant, which was established as the Priory Church in 1160. The nuns, 'The Ladies of Bungay', have long gone, and the Priory is now in ruins. Medieval Bungay was almost entirely destroyed in the great fire of 1688, which burned with such intensity that it is said to have melted the bells of St Mary's. The fire is commemorated by the domed Butter Cross, standing in a triangular market place in the town centre. Once produce was sold in its shelter, and it held a small cage where local villains could be locked up for public ridicule – hence the figure of Justice, sword and scales in hand, which surmounts it. A small market is held here on Thursdays. In the market place, a lamp post supports a weathervane in the form of the Black Dog of Bungay, popularly supposed to have been the Devil, who visited the town during a thunderstorm in August 1577 and killed two parishioners in the church. Bungay is the only town in England still to have a Town Reeve – an ancient office, dating back to Saxon times. There are many Georgian buildings, and the town is a pleasant and peaceful place – all the more so since the building of a by-pass which has spared the town centre from the worst of the hurrying traffic. Bungay can now afford to expand at its own pace.

TSB

Ipswich

Ipswich was one of the earliest Anglo-Saxon towns, and its port ensured prosperity through the Middle Ages. King John granted the town a Charter in 1200, and the splendid churches which survive from this period are an indication of the town's pride and importance.

The Ancient House dates from the 15th century, but in the 1670s it was given its oriel windows and wonderful pargeting showing the four continents – Australasia had yet to be discovered. Modern architecture is represented by the smoked glass of the Willis, Faber and Dumas building, and the futuristic shopping malls of Tower Ramparts in Tavern Street and the Buttermarket to the south of the town.

In the mid 19th century the port was given a new lease of life with the building of New Cut, a locked basin which enabled large ships to remain afloat whatever the state of the tide. The Custom House, suggesting a palace in the Italian style, was designed by a local architect, J M Clark, and opened in 1843. Beside it stands the modern Contship House, which has managed to retain some of the milling equipment from its former life, so work spaces are an interesting blend of old and new.

Christchurch Mansion stands amid varied parkland just a stone's throw from the central streets and squares. It was built by Edmund Withipoll, a successful Tudor merchant, on the site of the old Augustinian Priory in the space of just two years (1548–1550).

In 1735 the property was sold to the Fonnereau family, who were responsible for many of the splendid features. Their interest in it ceased in 1892 when a group of property speculators contemplated pulling it down in favour of a housing estate! Fortunately they were outbid by Felix Cobbold, a member of a local brewing family, and he presented both house and park to the borough. Within the Mansion today is an Art Gallery of outstanding quality, exhibiting works by Gainsborough, Constable and many more recent artists.

Eye

Eye is an unusual place. It is remarkable for its history, which shows it to have been an important market centre in the time after the Conquest; and perhaps even more remarkable now, when this small town – not much more than a village with its population of less than 2,000 – can stage an enormous summer spectacle, entertaining some 50,000 visitors in one weekend and presenting more attractions than any other such Show in the country. It is of course, ideally situated to attract most of Norfolk and Suffolk, being about half way between Norwich and Ipswich, and between Bury St Edmunds and the sea; but the ambitious idea of turning the former Eye Flower Show into an event where traders, military bands, steam engines, dog races and helicopter rides happily co-exist, is quite stunning. The Eye Show in its present form has been running since the 1970s, and it is growing every year. Preparations begin well in advance to ensure that each show is better than the last, with a variety of attractions to suit every taste. Held on a 75 acre site at Dragon Hill, just outside the town, the show combines trading tents and informative displays with spectacles such as stunt motorcycle teams, parachute jumps, hot air balloons and falconry demonstrations – even JCB diggers performing balletic dances. One year may see a cavalry regiment going through its paces, or a parade of vintage cars; the next may see a mock battle with a cast of thousands. Each show must involve a massive feat of organisation, all of which remains quite inconspicuous; there is a great deal of good natured fun, and all profits go to local charities.

The town has been shaped by two factors: its geographical position, on a sort of island (which is what the name Eye means) surrounded by low-lying, marshy land; and the castle, built here just after the conquest by William Malet, to whom the King gave the land. This gift comprised not only the village of Eye and the surrounding district, but the 'Honour of Eye', a collection of 247 estates. The castle built by Malet was the administrative headquarters of the entire area, and his son Robert established the market which grew up outside the bailey, soon becoming an important focal point for the surrounding farming communities. In the last 100 years fortunes have changed. The railway bypasses Eye, as does the main road; the market has dwindled almost to nothing, and the population has fallen. The centre of the town is occupied by a Victorian Town Hall, but there are plenty of pretty old houses in the narrow streets. The church tower is one of the wonders of Suffolk – over 100 feet high and panelled in flushwork. Next to it stands the 15th century Guildhall with its exquisite carved beams. Of the castle, little now remains, but it is sometimes possible to climb the castle mound and see a fine view of the town and surrounding undulating countryside.

Ickworth House

There are some buildings which, however magnificent and memorable, cannot hope to rival the story of the person most closely associated with them. Ickworth is such a monument.

Frederick Hervey was born in 1730, and in due course he entered the Church. His brother was Lord Lieutenant of Ireland, and so, in the time-honoured way, Frederick soon became Bishop of Derry. He showed a touch of the idiosyncracy which was to be his hallmark: he is said to have instituted curate races, whereby hopeful candidates for vacant parishes raced for the jobs on offer! He was so unconventional in Ireland that both Protestants and Catholics liked him.

Travel was his obsession, and soon he was touring Europe, indulging his love of art and architecture. After 1779, when he became the 4th Earl of Bristol, he visited the family estate at Ickworth, just outside Bury St Edmunds. He knew at once what he wanted to do – build a great house, to an original design, capable of displaying the cultural treasures he would acquire to fill it. He set off for Italy and there he met Mario Asprucci, an architect. The two began work on the Suffolk project, and as the design took shape the plans and instructions were sent to builders on the site. Incredibly, neither of them ever saw the house they were building in any other form than a papier mâché model! Clearly this was not the ideal way to work, especially as they were creating an innovative building, which presented practical problems to craftsmen hundreds of miles distant. While the work proceeded, the Earl-Bishop trawled the cities and palaces of Europe for examples of every type of art. He even bought things he personally disliked, but felt deserved a place in his collection.

The brilliant feature of his revolutionary design was that Ickworth was to have an enormous rotunda, containing the state apartments, while the art galleries would be placed at the ends of two great curved corridors, which would be lined with statuary. It would resemble a body with two great arms, as in an embrace. Such was his dream, but Fate had a shock in store.

When Napoleon conquered Italy in 1798, his army confiscated nearly all the Earl-Bishop's collection, and placed him in prison for nine months. On his release he attempted to resume his travels, and direct the work at Ickworth, but gout and exhaustion finally took their toll, and he died in a peasant's outhouse in 1803. He was not permitted to rest inside the house as he was considered a heretic. His body was ignominiously shipped back to England as 'antique sculpture'.

The great house was eventually completed, if not entirely to the original impractical designs, and today it contains many marvellous treasures, although most of them are not the product of those great European tours by Frederick Hervey. The National Trust is responsible for the house and gardens, so now at least there are thousands of admirers who have cause to be grateful to an eccentric 18th century Bishop.

Felixstowe

A few decades ago, the name of Felixstowe would have evoked a small seaside resort on the southern edge of Suffolk, whose sunny climate, safe shingle beach and beautiful seafront gardens attracted families for their annual holidays. So it still is; but for a new generation, Felixstowe is also the most successful container port in Europe, and the many thousands of ferry passengers who pass through it on their way to and from the Continent could be forgiven for not knowing that the other side of Felixstowe exists.

Felixstowe's development from a little fishing village into a prosperous port is largely due to the enterprise of Colonel Tomline, who bought a thousand acres of marshland on the northern bank of the Stour and proceeded to establish a rival to the port of Harwich on the opposite bank. Tomline improved access by building a railway line here from Ipswich, and the spa soon grew. A visit by the Empress of Germany in 1887 promoted the town's popularity, and at the turn of the century the mile long promenade was laid down and the pier built. The town has earned the name of 'The Garden Resort of Suffolk', and its seafront gardens rise in glorious tiers from the beach on the rather unpredictable crumbling cliffs. There is much to see and enjoy. The shops and businesses, perched on the cliffs, have a traditional air, and moves to pedestrianise the town centre have been resisted.

From the cliffs and the beach there is a superb view southwards across the estuary of the many dozens of ships which converge on the Haven ports. The fortunes of Felixstowe Docks rose and fell with the years, and by the 1960s the harbour had silted up and the jetty was dilapidated. Within a decade, however, Felixstowe had established itself as an independent port whose efficient handling techniques attracted much business. A new access road was built to Ipswich (with its road signs in several European languages), the port was greatly enlarged and ferry services introduced. It is now the country's biggest container port, handling millions of tonnes of cargo and containers each year. A viewing platform has been created beside the old Landguard Fort. Felixstowe is still expanding northwards towards Trimley Marshes, and a condition of its expansion was the creation of a reserve to protect the mudflats which provide feeding and breeding grounds for many migratory birds.

The Harvest of the Land

Although Suffolk has large towns and a diverse industrial base, it continues to be a county of small market towns, each closely dependent upon the surrounding farmland. With each passing year the number of agricultural workers is reduced. Villages which once supported shops, tradesmen and schools now have to make do with commuters and holiday lets. Strangely enough it is a story of progress and improvement: machines such as this combine harvester at Coddenham (*inset*), have liberated people from tedious, dangerous tasks, and advances in science and technology have brought into use land which had defied our forbears as being too difficult. In 1789 Ransomes of Ipswich began to make a superior cast iron plough, and throughout the next century Ipswich was supplying not just England but the Empire and beyond. At Leiston the firm of Garrett's specialized in threshing machines, and the manufacture of all the thousands of tools used on the land. Their catalogues were printed in four languages, and their portable steam engines can still be seen in the hands of proud enthusiasts at rallies and fairs.

The traveller likes farmland to be a pretty mix of wheat, woodland and flower-covered meadows. Farmhouses should not be spoilt by the presence of ugly hangar-like outbuildings, however useful they may be. Cattle and sheep are preferred to pigs and poultry, and a noble Suffolk Punch is appreciated too. But in the real world farmers grow what pays. Sugar beet has become a major source of income, once described as 'the solid lifebelt to which the drowning farmer could cling'. And at certain times of the year the great convoys of beet lorries converge on the factories in towns like Bury St Edmunds.

Everyone has become an expert on agriculture: we all have a view about EU agricultural policies and the effect they may have. What is more, farming is an uncertain business, and what makes sense in one year can mean ruin the next. We demand the highest quality food at the lowest possible prices, and yet feel uneasy as the human exodus from the land continues. Our love affair with the countryside has always been one of impression rather than fact – today we just find it harder to ignore the facts!

Mildenhall

One of the contradictions of this north-western corner of Suffolk is that it is now isolated and sparsely populated, whereas from earliest times it was in quite heavy occupation. In prehistoric times the flints of the nearby Breckland provided a ready source of tools and items for trade. The river Lark was used by both Romans and Anglo-Saxons and would have been the easiest highway for trade and communication.

Thistley Green is a small hamlet just outside Mildenhall, and in 1942 it was the site of one of the most important and spectacular treasure finds ever made in England. A farmer named Butcher was ploughing a field and when his tractor turned up some metal items which he knew would interest the landowner, he stopped digging and fetched him. Both men worked until it was dark, and when they had finished they had excavated 34 pieces, comprising plates, bowls and spoons. The largest plate was two feet in diameter. Mr Butcher knew nothing of their potential value and was content for his employer to take them home, and there they remained until 1946 when the local doctor chanced to spot an item, suggested that it was silver, and was told the story. The British Museum was informed. The pieces were all of silver, and careful cleaning revealed priceless and beautiful objects. A Treasure Trove inquest decided that the Roman owner had placed them in the soil with the intention of returning for them at a later time, and so declared them to be the property of the Crown. The four year delay prevented Mr Butcher receiving as much reward as would have come to him in 1942!

In November 1992 a retired gardener, Mr Eric Lawes, went into a friend's field at Hoxne, near Eye, to locate some lost tools with his metal detector. He found them, as well as a vast hoard of Roman treasure, comprising over 6,000 gold and silver coins, gold bracelets, silver bowls and about 100 silver spoons. It seems likely that these two Suffolk treasures were buried at about the same time, and for the same reason – Anglo-Saxon invaders were moving into the river Lark area causing panic among the Roman villa estate owners. When Mr Lawes cleaned out his car after all the excitement he found hundreds more coins!

Mildenhall is dominated by the church of St Mary and St Andrew, with its tower 120 feet high. Up until 1831 it even had a spire. Inside, the roof is a tribute to the craftsmen of the 15th century, and the angels which appear to support it survived even the gunshot of the Puritan desecrators of the mid 17th century. This is the largest parish in Suffolk, and in all directions the Fenland or Breckland landscape serves to heighten the sense of isolation.

Even the briefest visit to this very pleasant town will confirm that the USAF bases of Mildenhall and Lakenheath are very important to the area. Their high-tech aircraft contrast strangely with the idea of a Roman hastily burying his belongings in an adjoining field, but perhaps the timelessness of this region is one of its greatest qualities.

Blythburgh

There must be many thousands of people who have found themselves driving south along the A12, in the north of Suffolk, who have gasped to see before them the exquisite view of Blythburgh church across the vast flooded fields of Angel Marshes. Not for nothing is Holy Trinity Church known as the Cathedral of the Marshes – it soars above the small settlement and the inevitable question arises: why did a small village like Blythburgh need a church of such vast proportions?

Anna, King of East Anglia, was buried in the first church on this site. In 1130 Henry I founded a priory overlooking the river Blyth, and the beginnings of a quite prosperous era were evident. Ships tied up at the quayside, and wool and fish were bought and sold. The port grew in importance, and seemed destined to flourish. With this dream before them, the burghers of Blythburgh began an ambitious project in the early 15th century – the rebuilding of the church both to the glory of God and to the pride of themselves. Unfortunately, their crowning achievement was to mock their hopes, for as the glorious edifice was completed, the river silted up, and the ships were too large to navigate that far.

The church was for a time supported by the Priory, but when Cardinal Wolsey suppressed the Priory in 1528, Holy Trinity fell on hard times, and the building suffered from neglect. In 1577, during a great storm, the steeple collapsed, killing a man and a boy. During the Civil War, Dowsing, a Suffolk man, made one of his infamous visitations to stamp out Popery, and allowed his men to tether their horses in the nave, while they took pot shots at the splendid timber flying angels which support the roof beams. To add insult to injury, the churchwardens had to pay his costs!

Only in the 19th century did the church receive much needed attention: it was said parishioners sang in church beneath their umbrellas on rainy days. Today it commands awe and affection. The interior is vast, bathed in light, and leads the eye up to the angels, illuminated by the clerestory windows. At the west end of the church stands a Jack of the Clock, used to signal the start of the service. It dates from 1682, and has seen everything, including the recent tradition of a service of blessing for animals, from crabs, cats and guinea pigs up to the majesty of a Hereford bull.

Cavendish & Clare

There are many pretty villages in this part of the upper Stour valley, but surely none is more well-known and photographed than Cavendish. To be sure, the whole of the village is picturesque, with its well-tended gardens fronting old cottages and timbered inns; but the perfect view is acknowledged to be that from the village green, looking towards a group of pink-washed cottages and the church. The thatched cottages are in fact almshouses, collectively known as Hyde Park Corner; ruinous in the 1950s, they were restored, but subsequently burnt to the ground in a disastrous fire and rebuilt.

The 14th century church of St Mary was largely endowed by the Will of Sir John Cavendish, Chief Justice under Richard II, who in 1381 left the princely sum of £40 for the purpose. Unfortunately, this gentleman did not have a quiet end; his son had been one of those who had killed the rebel Wat Tyler, and as a reward the King promised to him and his heirs a pension of £40 for ever. But rebels in East Anglia were incensed at the death of their leader, and they captured Sir John and took him to Bury St Edmunds, where he was murdered.

The village has close by a prizewinning vineyard, based on a Tudor mansion. Along the village street, and just behind the duckpond, is the Old Rectory. There is also a fascinating museum detailing the history of the Foundation and its work today. All in all, the village is worth visiting at leisure.

The town of Clare is equally attractive, with a wide main street and the ancient church of St Peter and St Paul standing in a sort of island in the middle. Again, the houses all along the streets are picturesque, many of them having carved beams and pargetting. None is more beautiful than the Priest's House which stands next to the church. It dates from 1473 and now houses a museum. One of the emblems is the arms of the de Clare family. The manor of Clare was given to Richard Fitzgilbert, a knight of William the Conqueror, after the Battle of Hastings. This lord built a typical Norman motte and bailey castle nearby. Little now remains, as the de Clare family died out within 250 years, and later years saw the stones of the castle being used for local building by the townsfolk; only some stretches of wall remain on top of the 100 foot mound.

The whole area has for the last 20 years been a country park, with lakes and streams and a butterfly garden. Included in the park is the former railway station, built within the inner bailey in 1865 and closed just over 100 years later. The park warden now occupies the main station, and other buildings have a museum with models, displays and educational facilities. There are nature and history trails to follow.

Stoke by Clare is a pretty village with a grand house on the site of a priory. In the 18th century not one, but two, misers lived there, and the stories of their meanness may not be true, but they are entertaining!

Snape

The name of this small village means 'boggy place', and it seems that the settlement, originally at the head of the river Alde, moved on to higher ground because of the constant threat of flooding. Snape is only six miles from Aldeburgh and the sea, but by river it is 20 miles, winding between mudflats and tall reeds in a tortuous journey. It is a wild landscape, isolated and hostile; yet every year, visitors arrive by the thousand, as the Snape Maltings Concert Hall is renowned as the main venue of the Aldeburgh Festival.

Benjamin Britten, Peter Pears and Eric Crozier founded the first Festival of Music and the Arts in Aldeburgh in June 1948, as a showcase for contemporary work. It soon outgrew its original home in Aldeburgh's Jubilee Hall and even the large churches at Blythburgh, Framlingham and Orford, and in 1967 it moved to Snape, where Benjamin Britten had a home for a time in the Old Mill. Its new venue was the former Maltings, now converted to a concert hall. Two years later, the hall was destroyed by fire, but was re-opened within the year, and its magnificent acoustics make it the best in Europe.

The history of the Maltings goes back to the last century. A coal and corn merchant set up at Snape Bridge, and the premises were later taken over and converted into a Malthouse by Newson Garrett, grandson of Richard Garrett who founded the famous engineering works at Leiston. Garrett designed the buildings himself by drawing in the sandy earth with his stick (it is said that this accounts for their irregularity); and instead of simply exporting barley, he decided to convert it with the malting process, then ship it to London where his son managed a brewery. Modernisation brought the end of traditional malting in 1964, when the opportunity arose to buy these fine buildings. Now there are craft shops, restaurants and the Britten-Pears School for Advanced Musical Studies, and attractions all year round, including jazz and ballet. The conversion of the beautiful brick buildings is a work of art, lauded by many.

In 1862, the local archaeologist Septimus Davidson excavated one of half a dozen barrows on Snape Common and found the robbed grave of a wealthy East Anglian, in a 48 foot long clinker built long boat. More recently another barrow has been excavated, and the acid soil of this part of Suffolk has preserved its contents with intriguing results.

On the north bank of the Alde runs the Sailors Walk, followed by seamen returning to their ships at the coast. On the south bank lies Iken, the 'God forsaken and devil-possessed place' where St Botolph built his church in the 7th century. The present church, with its flint tower and thatched nave, is a landmark for miles around, rising over the blank saltmarshes. In 1968 sparks from a bonfire caught the roof and it was destroyed, but a dozen enterprising local folk have worked tirelessly to restore it to its former isolated glory.

The Museum of East Anglian Life, Stowmarket

Stowmarket is the ideal setting for a museum of East Anglian life, since it lies in the very heart of Suffolk. From earliest times the town was a trading centre; the river Gipping, and later a canal, provided access to Ipswich, and it has maintained its position as a centre for business, industry and shopping.

The Museum of East Anglian Life stands in farmland only a few minutes' walk from the market place. Since its foundation in 1904 the museum has expanded so that the site now covers some 70 acres. The exhibits focus upon the life of ordinary people, with particular emphasis on the 19th century. There are scenes from domestic life, with reconstructions of a typical house, and of shops such as existed within living memory but which have all but disappeared. We see an old Victorian schoolroom, complete with blackboard, easel and abacus. The industry of Suffolk is not neglected, and the museum has three steam traction engines as well as some static engines, locally built and now housed in the Boby Building. This impressive engineering workshop was originally from Bury St Edmunds; it now contains a number of small workshops where wheelwrights, basket weavers and coopers may be seen at their craft. The old Grundisburgh Smithy stands at the top of the Eight Acre Meadow; at the bottom winds the little river Rattlesden, and beside it are two mills – the Eastbridge windpump, and a watermill, resited here when Alton reservoir was created in the 1960s. Since agriculture has been so important to East Anglia, it is only fitting that one of the larger exhibitions should cover the farming year. The oldest building on the site, Abbots Hall Barn, is an enormous tithe barn dating in part from the 13th century, and it houses the collection of horse drawn vehicles. The Suffolk Punch is a breed esteemed for its power and good nature. In the heavier clay soils of East Anglia the Punch with its short 'feathers' at hoof was well suited, and although the numbers of these gentle giants dwindled at one stage almost to extinction, there are traditional farms where they may still be seen working the land as their ancestors did.

SOMES
RANSOMES
1953

Debenham

Near this pretty village is the source of one of the country's most beautiful rivers. The Deben rises in several ditches, flower-filled in spring and summer, but swollen in winter time with flood waters. The Anglo-Saxon 'deopan hamme' means 'deep and low-lying enclosure', and Debenham has Low Road, Water Lane and The Wash, where vehicles must splash through the Deben. Flooding has been a problem through the years; indeed, the Deben was perhaps once much deeper and broader, and may even have been navigable, since anchors have been found embedded in the ditch near Gull Farm. However, a 19th century scheme to re-open the Deben to river traffic was abandoned as unfeasible.

The district is now famous for its cidermaking; apple trees were imported for the purpose from Jersey in the early 18th century and modernisation allows many thousands of gallons of apple juice and cider to be produced every year.

The village has one main street. Cherry Tree Green at the south was once the site of the Cattle Fair and Lamb Show; to the north is Cross Green, and the High Street is broad and spacious. The church of St Mary crowns the gentle hill; its porch has some early Saxon work and was built like the fortress it sometimes became, with walls four feet thick and slit windows. The spire was struck by lightning and demolished in 1667. Nowadays all is harmony here, but in the last century it was reported that the church was kept 'in a very dirty state and did not appear to have been swept or cleaned out for several weeks'. A saying of 1642 ran 'High Church, Low Steeple, Drunken Parson, Wicked People'. During the Commonwealth, indeed, Debenham had no priest; banns of marriage were published on the Market Cross and weddings were conducted in the church porch by the Justices of the Peace. History shows the people of Debenham to be a spirited folk. In Jacobean times, a group of townspeople broke up a service and ousted the priest when he refused to read the revised prayer book. And it is said that Debenham men were renowned for their aggression, and would think nothing of walking to Framlingham for a good fight!

As in many old villages whose timber framed and thatched cottages stand close together, fire has been a great hazard, and has destroyed many of the more ancient buildings. In 1744 a great fire broke out at a bakery and destroyed a whole row of houses. In 1824 a collection was made for a fire engine – a 16 man manual, whose crew were alerted by the jangling of the church bells; but this did not prevent another big fire in 1849 when some fireworks exploded. But some things have not changed: in 1650 Timothy Abbott moved from Hadleigh to Debenham and opened a business as a cordwainer. The shop was handed down through the generations and is still thriving. Other old buildings survive, though in altered form, many with more modern façades, as in the case of the Guild Hall in the High Street, and altogether the village is most pleasing to the eye.

Southwold

Southwold lies in the heart of the Heritage coast, an ideal centre for holidaymakers; but although the population of the town almost trebles in the summer months, tourism has not really left its mark. This fashionable resort has retained an air of gentility, perhaps because Southwold has not compromised the natural attractions of the town and coast by introducing artificial entertainments.

Commerce centres upon the triangular market place. The houses and shops are largely Georgian or Victorian, and a pleasant walk will take in all the places of interest. First, the parish church of St Edmund, dating from the 15th century and a massive monument whose interior is unexpectedly light and airy. It has a magnificent painted screen, and 'Southwold Jack', a small wooden painted figure dressed as a soldier of the Wars of the Roses. He used to signal the start of a service by striking a bell with his axe. The church stands on Bartholomew's Green, one of nine such open spaces in Southwold – firebreaks created after the town was almost completely destroyed. The worst fire, in 1659, led to Southwold being declared a National Disaster Area.

Above the line of the rooftops near East Green rises the bright white tower of the Victorian lighthouse. It stands among the houses, away from the crumbling cliff edge, and has become the town's emblem. On East Green the smell of malt issues from Adnam's Brewery. The nearby Sole Bay Inn is named after a battle of 1672, also commemorated in the town sign. The cannon which now stand on Gun Hill, however, are quite unrelated to the battle; they are Elizabethan and were given to the town by the Duke of Cumberland in 1745 to help ward off pirates.

From here there is a spectacular view of the coast. Northwards, the cliffs slope down to where East Coast steamers used to tie up at the old pier. Now there is a grand new one, complete with an amusing water clock and hundreds of name plaques donated by generations of satisfied visitors. Southwards lie the common, the marshes and the River Blyth. Southwold was prosperous at the turn of the century when more than 300 herring drifters were based here. The large fish mart was affectionately known as the Kipperdrome. But the industry declined rapidly, and the track known as Blackshore skirts the now silted river where little boats lie at anchor, admired and envied by strolling holidaymakers.

The River Deben

Long before the existence of England, the East Anglians ruled themselves, and the greatest of their leaders was called Redwald. His palace was here at Rendlesham, and when the died in 625 AD he was brought down river to Sutton Hoo, the burial ground of his dynasty. An enormous rowing boat had been placed in a hole, and the body was laid in the centre, surrounded by the trappings of his status and wealth. A mound of earth covered the burial until 1939, when excavations revealed it to the world in all its splendour. An award-winning and successful National Trust museum now stands on the site and illustrates Anglo-Saxon life and culture – Page One of English history.

Woodbridge came into existence long after the last graves were dug at Sutton Hoo, and began its period of prosperity in the 15th century. Before this, the mouth of the Deben was the port area; the scores of creeks and inlets were given the name Goseford, and in their day saw fishing boats set off, invasion fleets at anchor, pirates preying on the unwary navigator and unfamiliar, curiously named vessels plying their trade. Even medieval kings knew of it, but the ships became too big, and the storms did their worst, and Goseford's loss was Woodbridge's gain.

For several centuries the Deben flourished as a ship-building river, with giant timbers being pulled to the yards of Woodbridge by horse teams. Eventually beautiful ships would move out into the main river, and sail off, probably for ever. Developments in ship-building killed the yards in the late 18th century, leaving only the humble working craft to tie up against small jetties, taking on grain or straw, and discharging coal or whatever made a tiny profit. Smuggling played a part in the local economy, and in the remoter stretches of the river there must have been stories both tragic and amusing with which to while away the nights at anchor, at places like Ramsholt and Waldringfield.

Today the river is still largely unspoilt, and only those afloat can fully experience its pleasures, for there are insufficient roads or bridges to bring the motorist within reach of all its treasures. Felixstowe, Waldringfield and Woodbridge have sailing clubs which ensure the river is respected and enjoyed.

Long Melford

Here is a village which merits its name: the main street is over a mile long, and broad. The inns, shops and houses which line it are an interesting mixture of Tudor, Georgian and Victorian and it is delightful to walk under the avenue of trees in such a delightful setting. At the northern end of the street, the ground rises and opens out to the most enormous village green, covering some 13 acres and ideal for village events such as the annual Bonfire Night display. Adjoining this on the western side is a line of pretty flower-bedecked cottages; opposite them is the splendid red brick of the Trinity Hospital, almshouses founded in 1573 for a dozen aged men by Sir William Cordell; and beyond is the magnificent church of the Holy Trinity, commonly thought to be the finest in the county. This church was built with the wealth brought to Melford by the cloth industry. It is bright and beautiful. The Lady Chapel is particularly so, with its interior cloister on three sides and its wonderful carved roof; for 200 years it was the public school for Melford. It was John Clopton of nearby Kentwell Hall who used his fortune to build the church; his tomb is to be found near the High Altar, as is that of Sir William Cordell. This latter gentleman, by profession a lawyer, rose to the position of Master of the Rolls under Queen Elizabeth I, whom he entertained at the Hall he built on the eastern side of the Green. Melford was once the hunting grounds for the abbots of Bury St Edmunds; in 1547, after the dissolution, Cordell was granted the Hall. There have been many changes to the Hall, but much remains. The high perimeter wall on the Green side conceals its beautiful grounds, including parklands, a sunken garden, a lily pond and topiary hedges, and in one corner is a fascinating octagonal summer house. Melford Hall passed eventually to the Hyde Parker family, who still live there. The National Trust has taken over its care.

To the north of the village lies yet another treasure, Kentwell Hall. It is approached down a long avenue of trees; pass through the gate and you are in fact emerging from a time tunnel into the 16th century, for here the Phillips family have taken the authentic setting and the equally authentic history of the Clopton family to recreate the Tudor world. Every summer hundreds of volunteers adopt the dress, manners, even the speech of that time, re-enacting a specific year in the history of this fine house. Here are all sorts and conditions of men, from the gentry to the serving maids. You will meet people at work: soldiers practising their artillery drills – the threat of a Spanish invasion was ever imminent – players rehearsing, musicians and calligraphers, dyers and weavers, bee-keepers and swineherds, herbalists and cooks. The inhabitants of this world express curiosity at the bizarre 20th century visitor – who feels out of place, as if it is he who is trespassing on their reality, and not they on his.

Bury St Edmunds

'Shrine of the King, and Cradle of the Law' is the motto of this West Suffolk town, and it neatly recalls two important events in its history. King Edmund was killed by the Danes towards the end of the 9th century, and when his body was brought to Bedericsworth it soon attracted pilgrims in large numbers. By the time of the Norman Conquest the town was called St Edmund's Bury, a fine Abbey was built in his honour, and his body was placed beside the High Altar in 1095. Until the 14th century St Edmund was the English Patron Saint, and so the influence and prosperity of the Abbey was enormous. It was at the High Altar in 1214 that a group of barons decided to confront King John, and within a year he had signed the *Magna Carta* – hence the town's motto.

But relations with the townsfolk were always strained, and in 1327 they burst into open riot, leading to the destruction of the Abbey. Nineteen people were subsequently executed, and a massive fine was imposed on the town. Rebuilding proceeded, and the Abbey Gateway, which dates from 1347, reflects the determination of the authorities never to suffer such an assault again, for it resembles a castle rather than the welcoming point of a religious order! Soon the Abbey enjoyed its former reputation for splendour and Leyland, who saw it in its prime, was moved to write: 'A man who saw the Abbey would say verily it were a city'. But the animosity between church and town was too deep to be forgotten, and when in 1539 the Dissolution occurred, the people were delighted, and no doubt gasped to behold the vast quantities of treasure that had been acquired over the centuries, now heading south into Henry VIII's greedy hands. The stone of the buildings was plundered freely, and just enough remains to suggest the sheer size of the great Abbey church. Houses have been integrated into the surviving flint arches of the West wall. When the diocese of St Edmundsbury was established, the nearby church of St James became the Cathedral, with an elegant spire added in the new century. The Abbey Gardens are beautifully maintained, and have won many awards.

Angel Hill which slopes towards the Abbey entrance, was until 1871 the site of a large annual market. Now it is a car park, overlooked by some of the best buildings in the town. The Angel Hotel, which is mentioned in *Pickwick Papers*, boasts a four poster bed used by Charles Dickens when he stopped in the town to perform a reading at the Athenaeum. This gracious meeting place for Bury society continues to dignify the town. Of a similar period is the Theatre Royal, which is a rare example of a Regency theatre, complete with intimate audience boxes and painted ceiling. It is now the responsibility of the National Trust. 'A handsome little town' was Dickens' verdict, and few would wish to quarrel with him. Cobbett wrote it was 'the neatest place that ever was seen', and it continues to provoke similar expressions of pride and pleasure.

YARMOUTH A143
MILDENHALL A1101
THETFORD A134
A14 IPSWICH
A14 STOWMARKET
A134 SUDBURY

Aldeburgh

Aldeburgh is a town which never loses its charm; whatever the season, it is delightful to breathe in the bracing sea air, or stroll along the broad High Street with its traditional shops. Life here is rather slow and old-fashioned, perhaps, but it is certainly genteel. The geographical isolation of Aldeburgh and its connection with music and the arts combine to create a delicate harmony which even the throngs of summer visitors fail to destroy.

The town's history is inextricably linked with the sea which has threatened its very survival. Once this was a fishing port and ship-building centre; salt pans provided that commodity to keep fish and meat wholesome. All this activity was centred upon Slaughden, where the river Alde meets the shingle spit and turns southwards for ten miles before finally reaching the sea. But Slaughden as a village no longer exists; it was taken by the hungry sea in the early years of last

century. Of medieval Aldeburgh, little now remains. The 16th century Moot Hall once stood in the town centre; now it is prominent on the sea front, only yards from the concrete wall which protects the town in time of flood. Nearby is a children's boating pool, and, overlooking it, the statue of Snooks, a memorial to two local doctors, in the form of their little dog. Dr Nora Acheson had the distinction of being the only woman to accompany the lifeboat crew on missions, until forbidden by the RNLI as it was too dangerous. Aldeburgh is rightly proud of its lifeboat, housed in a fine, modern boathouse at the top of the beach, ready to be launched into the crashing waves.

The church of St Peter and St Paul, set on high ground, has a plaque to the memory of the crew of the *Aldeburgh*, the lifeboat which capsized on duty in 1899 with the loss of seven men. In a chapel is a bust of the poet George Crabbe. It was his poem *The Borough*, depicting Aldeburgh and its inhabitants, which was the inspiration for another genius associated with the town: Benjamin Britten lived in Crabbe Street for ten years and composed *Billy Budd* and *The Turn of the Screw* here. John Piper's commemorative window enlivens the church with its bright colours; Britten is buried in the churchyard beyond. His real memorial, perhaps, is the Aldeburgh Festival which he founded in 1948, and which within a few years outgrew its birthplace and is now housed in the famous Snape Maltings Concert Hall, upstream on the river Alde.

LT336

Sudbury

Sudbury is one of those towns in the southern part of the county whose population has more than doubled over the last 50 years, so that the visitor is aware of modern housing and shopping developments; but the hub of the town is still the Market Hill, where St Peter's church overlooks a wide open space flanked by fine buildings of grey and red brick, and on market days, when traffic is banished, it is easy to see how Sudbury maintains its position as a busy trading centre.

Sudbury was the biggest of the weaving towns, and some of the finest buildings date from those prosperous times. In Stour Street are the best examples, Salter's Hall and the Chantry, with their carved beams and traceried windows. Flemish weavers were settled here by Edward III, and later the town diversified into silk, satin and velvet weaving. There were as many as 600 silk looms at one time. The river Stour was made navigable in the early 1700s and although the last barges made their way downstream in the first part of the century, today's visitors can take a short steamboat ride from Sudbury Quay, or walk across Friars Meadows or Freeman's Great Common to experience the beauty of the Stour at this point. But a glance at the records shows that the town is very ancient. It is well situated in a defensible position in a loop of the river Stour, and was fortified during Saxon times – the curve of Friars Street follows the line of the defences. The oldest church is St Gregory's, mentioned in Domesday; that is set to the north of the town in a wide open space called the Croft. It was rebuilt by Simon of Sudbury, who was Archbishop of Canterbury under Richard II, and notoriously unsympathetic towards the peasantry, whom he called 'barefooted rebels.' He established a savage poll tax, so it is not surprising that he was one of the victims of the Peasants' Revolt; his severed head was brought back to the town of his birth and his skull is kept in the vestry of St Gregory's.

Undoubtedly, however, Sudbury's most famous son is Thomas Gainsborough. He was born in the town in Sepulchre Street (now renamed Gainsborough Street), just off the Market Hill in 1727, in a house still standing and which has now become an art gallery. The house itself looks Georgian, but the red brick façade was added by Gainsborough's father, a wealthy weaver, to a pair of medieval houses. Inside you will see some of Gainsborough's paintings set in simply but elegantly furnished rooms. Gainsborough showed early talent and was sent off to London in his early teens, but he returned to Sudbury, a married man, in 1746, and settled in Friars Street where he and his wife brought up their two daughters. Gainsborough's fame lies in his portraits, but he always professed that his first love was landscape painting, and declared 'Suffolk made me a painter.' Sudbury is rightly proud of its famous son, and it is a bronze statue of Gainsborough, palette in hand, which presides over the market place as if serenely observing the bustling activity of the scene.

Framlingham Castle

Castles were built to control territory, and protect their garrisons from surprise attack. During the troubled times of the Middle Ages traders came to appreciate the security to be found in the shadow of a castle's fortifications. At Framlingham the modern town is actually closer to the castle than appears to be the case: there was a large bailey and a walled lower court. The ditches to these features may still be seen, and emphasize how thoroughly the planners had prepared their defences.

Roger Bigod began constructing the present castle in 1190, and in its day it was a revolutionary design, for it forsook the conventional plan of a keep surrounded by a curtain wall, and went instead for a fortified curtain wall, dependent for its defence on a series of towers. The towers are open at the back and would have had removable timber bridges across them; thus an attacker gaining access to the wall walk would be unable to make much use of his advantage, and a 40 foot drop was the price of failure!

Above the gate tower it is possible to see the holes through which the drawbridge chains passed, and the slit which once housed the mighty portcullis. The gaps in the walls are called crenels, and they were protected by wooden shutters which tilted just sufficiently to allow an archer to make a shot. Both crossbows and longbows were provided for, as shown by the varying apertures of the slits.

The ditch was always dry, but no less of an obstacle for an attacker. On the west side there are the tall pillars which once supported a bridge dating from the time when the castle became a hunting lodge, and so it enabled horsemen to ride into the surrounding parkland without troubling the townspeople. Most of the brick chimneys, which are fakes, date from this period, and they were thought to improve the appearance of the property! The visitor approaches the castle gateway over a solid bridge, but that dates from Tudor times, when the castle became one of the residences of the Howard family, who were Dukes of Norfolk. Several of the family are buried in St Michael's Church, beneath magnificent monuments. In 1553 the castle saw its most famous visitor make history, for it was here that Queen Mary was proclaimed sovereign, refuting the claim of young Lady Jane Grey.

In its heyday the main courtyard would have been like a farmyard, with animals, smells and outbuildings everywhere. Now the scene is one of green lawns, flowers and a pretty stone hall. This building was once the town poorhouse, but today it contains a shop, the town museum and an exhibition space.

The walk up to the wall platform and the view from the wall itself are not to be missed, for the castle exactly fits our expectations of a medieval fortification. In all directions the view is worthwhile, and during the summer the courtyard below offers a varied programme of operas, plays, concerts and even medieval combat.

Chelsworth & Monks Eleigh

The writer Julian Tennyson described Chelsworth as his favourite Suffolk village, and it is easy to see what attracted him to it. The houses are all beautifully preserved, and flowers seem to cling to every beam and post. All the houses seem to be on the same side of the street, allowing everyone to enjoy the uninterrupted pleasure of looking across fields at agreeable rural activities. Once a year almost every garden opens its gates to visitors, in aid of charitable causes, a sure indication that this is a village which takes its appearance very seriously. The river Brett is crossed by a double hump-backed brick bridge and the scene is made even more enticing in spring when the water meadows are festooned with waving daffodils. The view from this spot is breathtaking and few visitors would quarrel with the proposition that this is one of Suffolk's loveliest quiet places. The Norman church of All Saints sold all but one of the bells in 1746, so today's bell ringers perform at a disadvantage!

The village green of Monks Eleigh is so perfectly peaceful and traditional that it seems to lack for nothing, but investigation reveals that it lacks the presence of monks! There never were any here, despite the name. The first lords of the manor were called Illeigh, and they held the estate from the monks at Canterbury, who doubtless were interested enough to collect their rents, but not enough to live among the tenants. The church of St Peter dates from the late medieval period, and once it had a spire, but it was removed in 1845 when it became too dangerous. The village green has a curious pump, and pretty cottages lead the eye to the fine church. This scene once appeared on railway posters and helped to popularize the village idyll.

Nearby is the village of Bildeston, which contains many superb timber framed houses, some of them leaning alarmingly off centre, but no less secure for centuries to come, such is the wonder of wood as a building material! Wool was the source of riches throughout this part of Suffolk, and Bildeston's particular gift was to produce good quality blankets. St Mary's Church stands outside the village, overlooking the huddled houses of the centre. It is quite likely that the original village was centred on the church before the ravages of the Black Death in the 14th century. In 1975 the tower was blown down in a gale.

Suffolk Churches

Suffolk has more churches per square mile than any other county, and almost 400 of them were in existence at the time of the Domesday Book (1087). Many stand on sites which go back to the very beginnings of Christianity in East Anglia. In AD 601, Pope Gregory urged his monks to build on pagan sites, hoping that they would effectively suffocate the primitive faiths they displaced. Ellough near Beccles means 'heathen temple', and at Iken, beside the river Alde, there is a church on a site which is believed to go back to Roman (Iceni) times.

The great age of Suffolk churches, the 14th and 15th centuries, came about because wealthy benefactors believed that if they devoted their fortunes to the praise of God they might just avoid eternal damnation. In Lavenham, seen here, the Earl of Oxford and the clothiers of the Spring family lavished money on the church, making both a political and personal statement by doing so. This was the period when churches gained their stained glass, clerestories, magnificent roofs, towers and porches. Blythburgh, Southwold, Needham Market, Long Melford, Mildenhall, Lakenheath and scores of other fine buildings bear witness to the generosity and importance of individual donations, often the fruits of trade, fishing or agriculture.

Intolerance and bigotry have left our churches scarred and incomplete: William Dowsing, the Puritan, actually kept a diary of the churches he desecrated, often remarking how many statues and windows he had smashed in a single day! (He needed two days to visit all the Ipswich churches.)

Within the churches of Suffolk there are a multitude of pleasures, treasures and some surprises. At Wenhaston the churchwardens had whitewashed the late 15th century 'Doom', or Day of Judgement painting. Fortunately an accident of rain exposed the work in the 19th century and it was restored. At Wingfield John de la Pole, who sought the throne itself, has finally found peace, while at Framlingham the Earl of Surrey, poet and courtier, has time to reflect on the injustice of his execution by Henry VIII. Dennington has the beautiful monuments to Lord and Lady Bardolph (inset), a fitting resting place for him after the confusion of Agincourt. Every Suffolk church richly repays the time and effort of study, for they are a microcosm of a community which extends across more than a thousand years.

Walberswick

The village sign of Walberswick is a wrought iron design of a ship, and this is most appropriate, since the sea created Walberswick's period of greatest prosperity – and was responsible for its decline. Nowadays this pretty village is quiet, undisturbed apart from the summer visitors and the seabirds, but once it was a major fishing port, with 13 barks plying as far north as the Faroes and Iceland, and 22 inshore vessels.

Access to Walberswick is restricted. For the walker there is a picturesque approach from Southwold, crossing the bridge upstream of the rickety wooden jetties which jut out into the river Blyth. But for the motorist there is only one road, across the heathland from Toby's Walks, just south of Blythburgh. Before reaching the village, the tower of the church of St Andrew can be seen; poverty caused it to be cut short, and the eastern end of the nave is an ivy clad ruin. Walberswick has had to contend with a number of disasters down the centuries. The sea has inundated the village on many occasions. A high earthen bank has been built to protect those houses at the northern end, and marram grass planted to stabilize the sand dunes; nevertheless, erosion of this part of the coast progresses at an annual rate of more than a metre. Fire, too, has wreaked havoc here on more than one occasion and reduced the population to penury. In spite of misfortunes, a small remnant remained to keep the village alive. Today Walberswick has only one professional fisherman, and the Fishermen's Flats, where nets were once spread to dry, is a car park. The fish warehouses on stilts may still be seen by the water's edge, and the ferrywoman will row passengers across the river to the Southwold side; but the rail link with Southwold has long since disappeared. The train used to cross an enormous swing bridge over the Blyth at a speed of 16 mph. In the summer you had time to jump out and pick flowers from the bank and then jump back in again! Nowadays visitors come here to enjoy the walks across the saltmarsh where villagers grazed their geese and cattle, and families appreciate the beautiful long beach of fine white sand. This is also the venue for the annual Crabbing competition – a national event which attracts many contestants.

Front Cover Photograph:
WOODBRIDGE TIDE MILL
Back Cover Photograph:
SAXTEAD GREEN WINDMILL